COMMONSENSE OF THE SENSES

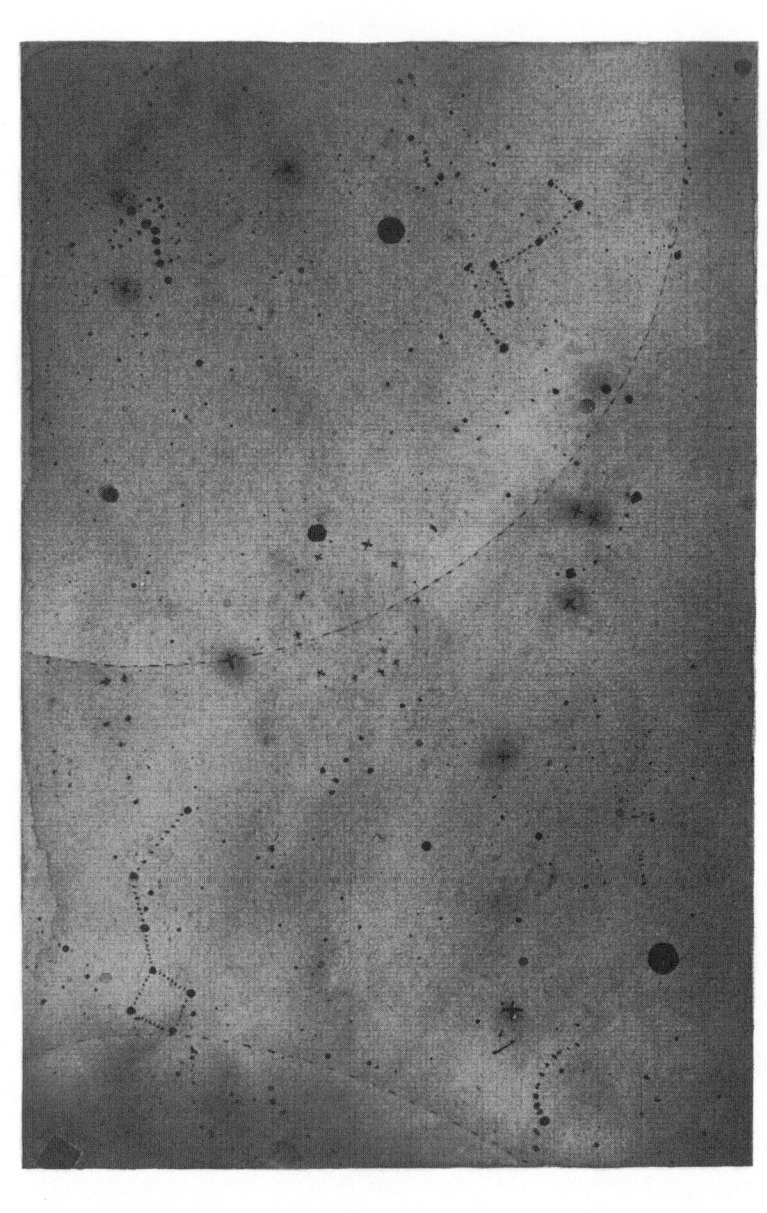

Commonsense of the Senses

sequence of poems
(1978-1980)

by
JONATHAN GRIFFIN

THE MENARD PRESS
1982

COMMONSENSE OF THE SENSES

Grateful acknowledgement is made to Montemora (New York)
where some of these poems first appeared

ISBN 0 903400 79 0

The Menard Press is a member of ALP

Illustrations by Julia Farrer

Menard Press books are distributed in North America by SBD:
Small Press Distribution, 1636 Ocean View Avenue, Kensington,
Cal. 94707, USA.

The Menard Press
8 The Oaks
Woodside Avenue
London N12 8AR

Printed by Skelton's Press,
Wellingborough, Northamptonshire

. . . the mystery is
That there is something for us to stand on.

GEORGE   OPPEN

I am deeply grateful to the painter, Julia Farrer, for having created the illustrations to this book.

Each of these poems is meant to work and please on its own; but they also interact, and the book as a whole, if read straight through (not necessarily at one go), yields a firmer meaning.

The lay-out of the poems is not random: it contains a simple notation, useful in reading aloud. A line with 5 stresses starts fairly near the left hand edge of the page, one with 4 stresses further to the right, one with 3 the same distance further, and so on: a reader who is unsure how many stresses to make in a line has only to observe where it begins.

This system of indentation is maintained strictly. Some other (and normal) expression-marks, such as breaks in a line (its later part or parts placed lower than the preceding) or enlarged spaces between lines or between words, are also used, but freely, as the poem has seemed to require.

J.G.

CONTENTS

1

See the skimming
honeycombing
Sun
       brimming
the cloud glades'
colonnades

as far as eyes can see

Know the creeping
many groping
scums
       seeping
the ways through
all the blue

as far as air can be

WHERE

        Backs to the wall?
          this

          is edge –
          the abyss
          touch

        Backs to the fall

To perceive is to seek: nostrils clutch
scents, eye-orbs scan, a hand encircles things,
hunger and hunt   race   teeth-palate-tongue,

while the mysterious ears sit still
(never, even in a sleepfast head, shut) –
holding out quietly two shell-like coils
for meanings maybe warnings which the skull's
electric clocks measure as tones like colours.

It is, I know, humanly possible
to love a desert – not all Earth one desert;
to love the Dead Sea – not   every sea dead.
To love a desert, one must know
                                    of leaves
cropping, and that there is a sea with lives.

Young man, young woman, be the Green Apostle

BRINGING DOWN

On three sides precipice –
if we do not pull up we shall
fall
into the Universe

and bring down all
the temperate globe's inventive life

all
stifled
in the between fires
abyss

Earth
Beth-
lehem of the Universe

breath
birth-
place of the innocents –

these we take to death

Thee we take to death

Omnipotent?　　how, if
the Universe is out of
control? amok except that gravity
　　　　　　seems to be holding

　　　tautly　　certain harmonies
– bulges of rout – local coherences –
the solar system and those superclusters
　　　　　of galaxies

　　　Intergalactic gravity –
　　　　　　source
　　　　　　some
　　　dark imagined mass
hidden in the open by its stars?

MANENS MYSTERIUM

Credulity
is blasphemy

The horses of the Universe are bolting

Everybody has need of some religion
to make him/her
                    part of a Sense beyond
day-to-day material competition

but claim contact with a God having in hand
            the stampede Universe
astrophysicists are revealing to us?

            that? when there is – look, here
beyond/at hand – Earth   alive   dear

      She is holy – and at our mercy
      She is Goddess   in our care
To save Earth-the-Sense-of-the-Universe
can give a sense to our lives – alone can –
            can now   here
                        since from ourselves
      the life of Earth has to be saved

MINIMAL CREED

                  If
            the Universe
      has

          a sense
                     it's
          Earth

          I believe
          may have

FATHERLESS

A traveller to London caught by night
two hundred years ago rarely saw a light:
dropped into now . . . *Where? Heaven! . . . Babylon?*
The ceremonial ways
                    blaze
                        on and on

Showery night, clouds flushed with the diffused
luxury – streets' gold waste noticed by few . . .

Along reaches of roofs waterglints tingle –
at windows the dawn is fumbling sand fingers

Men and women of the prodigal cities!
that there is God to forgive terracide is
doubtful   and it's hard to get unkilled

        Look about in the strict light
        Change waste to trees before too late
The death of Earth has now to be unwilled

Moon!
death!

reminder
to deaf
Belshazzar Man
– not also blind –

inspire the
fear of the death of Earth

The repeating graffito hallows
the heavens wall

MAN!

LEARN
TO LOVE:
LIVE
IN FEAR

OF EARTH'S
DEATH
NEAR

2

WHILE THERE IS SOIL

               Out walking
                             mind
         hoarding trees
                   for their approaching
            rarity value

FOR A TIME STILL

     A winter woodland filled with even halflight
         Warm
                    down here in the windless wood
 listen!
       the wood's wires   out in the wind

Brought up to think 'self' is a dirty word
       – it is a sacred one:

this soul my hands of mind scoop from the Moon
       I will   call my own

       Word to not be profaned

right hand to write
       on the wall
         WE ARE WARNED

POMP

          No Moon no cloud   night
          gorgeous with stars only

          measureless golds scarce light
               showing up Life
               the Rare
                       lonely

THE SAVING SCORN

We wake   under the eyes of the dream

     They turn away in disdain
     What did – do we seem?
     We look for them in vain

O children we are robbing! turn away!
          may
we   have left you not just dirt and dearth
          on scrap-heap Earth
but each of you the proud eyes of a dream

PART ATONEMENT

Even Jesus can't
shame   God to repent

but human beings?
                              my
work   needs to be good enough to atone to
posterity for what – their substance – I
waste: have my work cut out until I die

It is the quality
matters High quality makes quantity
also count
A first-rate
artist ought to create
of things better than him enough for some to
outlast vandals to come

Art is
just
the best

on offer
to
        whoever
will
        aspire
to be its peer

Has to
be earned
Its givers own it

All
who made it
or heard it call

obeyed
relayed it –

who earn it
own it

THE SLUNG BRIDGES

Poetry's teaching: To take words as meaning
what they say – especially when they mean
something else   To take the words as meaning
all they say
                    and suspend   tracks between

BECAUSE AND DESPITE

Dante   lyric poet, epic theme –
                    with him,
            strung along
the cosmic structure, bloom-clusters of song:

Pound   lyric poet, epic plunge – the Cantos
            shine now and then with Sapphic splinters.

TO THE POINT

A poem's not about the wood, or trees –
it is about a tree
                    and through that trees's
            roots   has in it Earth
and through the bole and boughs and leaves of one
tree   holds the sky and pulls the Sun
                    eats light   creates breath

Music raises façades serene
with interfenestrations of
the plain stone of silence
These receive
all vicissitudes of light
with variations on their own
deportment of delight

From the dust of the boulders whose fall killed
the gods
        may my
               tears and hands wash some gold

A poem her own lie-detector

Thingward bound –

trying
feigning as corrector
of feignings and,
the Thing Light found,
seeing –

poetry is a person being
simple without lying

3

Moments in the Bible are haunted places –
you come to sudden chill
                        Problem of Evil
no pretence of solving take it or leave it
appears   as a myth   – that is   naked

The Holy Innocents
                        Noah drunk   naked
because *the Lord*   *shut him in* in the faces
drowning
            Job's children and their servants take it . . .
And now I feel what sort of place this place is

Here   It   in *us* deep through us snowing
and suddenly we are where we are going –

in   the greed of Man and will not leave it:
have seized all Earth are making Earth too small
to feed all – fouling Her – And we spill soil

We have come to the place It is us   evil

Establishing the text of the Universe
to read its meaning and not read a meaning
    into it
      and yet
  how fill the lacunae?

    obstinate sail
marring the desolation with a soul
  out in the desolation sane

    manned
    unsound

FALL COMPLETED

Man   barred from Eden
        found   the other
                forbidden
tree – the animal branches
tree of life   mother

        Her blood nothing
        now   stanches

                Earth
                bleeding
                to death

ACCOMPLISHMENT

I was a child when sea was clean

We had room I
                    have seen
this earth the sweet rose of the Universe
– during youth I breathed the maiden of air

Soon now I'll die knowing that I have been
Man   fouling to death the One And Fairest

TRUTHTIME

> I dread yet hunt truth
> to the edge of dread's lying
>
> Am not afraid of dying
> Am frightened of death to Earth

There a forgotten current, having crawled
        along profound mudflats
lit solely by their denizens' errant lights,
is crowded upwards
                and brings killing chill
        to frontier waters where the filtered
        Sun's reach   seasonally falters

        and while the sway of the Moon still
with invisible strings pulls at it all,
expanding and contracting limbs of cold
                rise
                        dilute
        slowly
                        until
a monster sloth turbulence floats   sprawled

GOD AND EVIL

> *a father should leave*
> *his grown*
> *child alone*
> *stop it*
> *being his own*
> *a puppet*

If the child   will
          level
the house   kill
          itself
and risk   all
things that live?

Man the Overkill –
can Man-greed be God's will?

the major evil, Man,
irradiates   fouls
air   sea   soil –
                fells
        life itself

Hard to see how one can
choose   Man's survival

BUT THEN?

Stripped, recognised, the reasons for despair
— we start there

Stay where we were?

If you move aside
still it points at you

My gaze, steer into the Moonseed –
sail up the estuary
the Moon has thrown silver between
forest shores of sea

never attain
the eyeless hinterland
it signs
to

IN SOULS' DROUGHT —

poet mind, diviner —

poised on a thumb-ball the divided
hazel twig   waiting to twitch
at some   trickle buried
                          within
                this dust
                this thirst
                this parching
                search

Here stone walls built by men to keep
not men out but (more or less) sheep
in   co-operate with the structural
rock —
     having earned, challenge
                equal
footing with the swell of the hills

establishing the moors scale

Against distance
rarest nears

let each soul-instant have
the retained toing & froing
a wave is
        record of
much loyal coming & going

    soul   -   instants
    among light-years

AFTER DESPAIR

It seems there was a purpose in the night

hysteria cured
                        by the agony it was flight
from
        coats your waking soul with dust of light

In   the light which holds the stars lost in it –

NOBLESSE OBLIGE

Nobly bound to maintain their energy
steadfast at high availability
there is
            a selfmade aristocracy –
those who hold off and drive back entropy

REARGUARD ACTION

The whole countryside set ablaze with trees

the fired stores of an army in retreat

Each autumn this defiance in defeat

FIRST AND FAIREST

While still the oaks and elms
stand stiff in brown habits of poverty
still ready patiently
to heave the sap
their long ways up

Look!   here come
snowdrop and crocus alms

('73, '79)

The gentle rise
                    breaks – here we halt
                                        above
the stepping sea the shuffling of the surf –
look down into the February wind
            that's bent up by the cliff –

three yards from the edge
                        sit
                            feeling the Sun
            and breathing warm grass scent
        and hearing now and then the sound

Over reefs-of-woodland hedgerows
the wind curls

Overhanging shadow-whirls
sunlit sprayfray edges rise

Thing-leaves
thought-branches –
ranges
of lives

Heather, peat, rock

In a safe crook
the tarn

brown
heifer eye

deepens a blue of sky

Wide vineyards, sun – the valley a vat of silence
filled with only the lowing of the vines

I heard with eyes that held my breath
this milk the valley had filled with

And still I stood and by turns with
joy breathed the scent, awe held my breath

They have no voice but heaviness the vines'
loaded udders   Lowing-for-hands silence

VERGE

Soft sounds that fend off silence
yet have   virtue of silence

whispers between kisses
                    when whispers question
        and silence answers
                            lips mingled
    four   lips in a kiss singled

POMANDER

> Healer of faith to youth, reminder
> not to grow old,
> apple-of-amber love – pomander
> in the fouled world

VERWEILE DOCH

> The wind has made her hair his own
> it darts to catch him
>   he is gone
> It droops   now
>   and dreams alone –
> no, look! Again –

LEFT OPEN

Is this the hiss of loss of God which we
receive from
                all the stars not even Hell?

What sounds do dead men's ears catch, as a shell
that's lost its beast holds the roar of the sea?

DAYDREAM OF FORGIVENESS

I heard
      a fall of silence
               the end of all when
the dying fall has died   silence fallen

        falling still

LIGHTWEIGHT

I can't write about other people's deaths
      About my own I can   with
some hope
        which outweighs the fearwisps and where
the weight is
         doubt – the hope there's nothing there

      a weight of wings
             holds up and breathes

'Fear God' says Hermes Trismegistos 'God
is a man's natural strength, and company
to the lonely   whoever he be' Indeed
fear: God is the loneliness of the lonely –

God is what drops a man when he is lonely
the grey day of the soul is at last God:
        one is alive and dead,
among the stars Man killing Earth – that only . . .

        Suddenly maybe meeting
true eyes – a visage creased by love – a self
whole: heart of grace keeping body and soul,
        even to the most thin
capillaries of the mind, holily beating . . .

the circulation of the light within

4

&

Shimmering of wings sea,
Holy Spirit moonglade!
                    seek

– living silver ampersand!
      Spirit seen! –

twine, into mercy trinity,
death's-head Moon
                    &
                    monished me

WILL

The flame stands up
                    stands almost still
        not free and yet freestanding
a standing stone of flame
                        implying

fire-sarsen henges of free wills —
half-transparent poles with standards
        up-held and while held flying

The falling grey
— moved away —
declares surrender
by a rainbow

Raindrops have found
near the ground
a new thing

    green

to which they cling
— quickly their own
doomed prisms sing
O Offspring
of Her   Spring

PRESENT

From a tree – one –
I have the Sun

I feel an apronful of fruit
– the weight of light –
                              pull my arms (tied
forwards by a loved load) taut

to save the Sun this tree has bought

Live in the present? – stand   in
a point   ever?
                    On
                       and on

          Or if

                       when
                    looking at one
          thing   or breathing music in
                    through ears and the throats of one's skin
                    the thirst of the tuned skin
                       or springing
                                   living
          in   the point of giving

The woundless dead
have blue blood

Half-lives' blood
a dull blue?

The dreams of the true
noble are fed
by throbbing red

made in the white
hollow bones' night
and, shut in, driven
through   labyrinth

keeping faith
to the extreme
capillary thinths –
there
    blued
until restored,
driven through
     breath
     to red

    the stream
keeping faith
undoing death

Now twinkling eyes spill smiles along the sly
wrinkles which
                      as though channels for that dry
irrigation
          slowly were riddled by
assiduously the quick swiveling sphincters

And wisdom twinkles, little though we know:

is eyes cleared by the doubt blink: is the slow
metaphysics from swiveled wonder – crow's-
feet flanking quick old eyes –
                     a thinking, sphinctral

Hard mind
diamond

lucid water
darting fire

can cut fetters

May shut fetters,
show fair the fair:
doubt   can unbind
then unblind,
and truth turn doubt
inside out

to – if not faith –
at sight allegiance,
love!
           Of Earth

A life's obedience

Love

carved

the baboon of Ripon choir – love, carved

MAELSTROM

Mother of every Spring   choked Mother
– us choking Her and choking in selfsmother –

we are alone with mocked posterity

            The mocking open beckons me
            the vortex future sucking me

Earth is the place where one world mocks another

The first lie hissed from the ore tree –
the fruit

was not
knowledge of good and evil: the gift of Eve is
the good and the evil of   knowledge except
of good and evil

So
Eden
lost for – ? original temptation even
not true?

Or
(hindsight if that)
the wrong fruit
kindly forbidden

for
evil of knowledge has
taught us at late last
what is   good and what is   evil Now
we bloody know

The tree-dappled white quadrangles of Heaven
                     are weeping from all angels
paradisal resins of charity over
               Her Whom Man is ageing

A poet – unincarcerable mind
whose longing is to be just, not to judge –
must
      in the crowd greed here at Plunge Edge
judge
      and plead with / against
                        vandal mankind

Calabria '78, a jotting:
An Italian hill city
now has below it several glittery
screes of trash.

The glitter of the litter
fracturefresh
the cachinnation of the jettisoning:
the irreversible frivolous sinning –
Man wasting Earth
in heartless mirth
Blasphemy Man building
Earth's obsolescence in . . .
'God made Man in His image' God is greed?

Trust in the mercy of Greed! let us pray *Greed*
have mercy on us! Have mercy on Earth, O Greed!

We are in greed's Hand
Let us pray Man we have to

WAR ROOM

The admiralty in the small skull manned
by the left-handed mirror-writing mind
shall work its great fleet – keep mapped
(the plotted light-dots citying the dark screen
truth at a glance) each sloop each submarine

and, through communication's throbbing web
(deceptive stillness talking), hold them apt
to muster hover swoop wherever willed

– policing all the waters of the world?
Who shall police the police? Discontrolled
– stillness crushed – a civil-war-room! filled
to bursting by one inter-mutinous crew
wrecking! Obsession – craw to crazing craw
until the seas die of the waste we strew

THE KNOWLEDGE

The schizophrenia of an ocean – stretched
twisted – pegged down between Earth Moon and Sun
by its own weight   while by the storms' boots torn
travelling gashes mock the main tide-stress:

a brain's dignity – soft crinkles compressed
motionless, holding unseen ocean tension
in the world flood of greeds which (it knows) soon
must, numberblinded, be Earth's death unless.

Knowledge of good and evil is the worst
test – the jagged shocks and smooth shame twist,
waste, can dis-soul a soul: to live and have
        left – regarding good and evil –
              no mistaking Henceforth
                 knowledge, not faith

We breathe the fall-out of our folly
deep
    and about
        and desecrate
      the marrow Holy of Holies

till *we*
    fall out –
        irradiate
arteries   of the will-   be-
    born with the white blood fate

    Greed in the air
  death in young bones we are

SENSELESS

i.m. M.K.

The suicide
let the black star
take his future

Earth has bred
– on Herself fed
the terracide

Rebirth within the ice siege
stubborn summer
                    At the fiord's edge
willows five inches tall in brief
full leaf weeping   as if watching
                the bergs marching
forth   smoothly towards a warm
                    doom
Higher up, yellow poppies give
glows here and there to slopes of silver
Out from rock nooks saxifrage plucks
            courage to dare the open

        And there are gentians peeping
        – then sudden bold blue fills
        dwarf meadows deep with hope

        In long shadows the floes
        stay   dead   grey

        Soon again nothing
not grey or white
                save where, to North,
        elfin algae redden
        unsubdued snows

            Life
                    fight on
            against Man

In this book the word Thee
      is used
  once
     – addressed
to not   God   Whose
  existence is vague
but Goddess Earth   Hers
  being evident

To God some prayers are sent
  provisionally

  urgently

Must Earth require of me
  prayers for plague?

(*added*, '82)

We   whose procreance recruits
Children Crusaders of the future –
we the to be extinct salute you . . .

exploded Colosseum!   mute
sparkling backs
            of the stars   fugitive!

No response   just that faint hiss

and we out here on stage to face
the claws   ours, terracides' remorse,
and – to the remnant soil – confess . . .

      We pray   but the mercy
          has
          to be ours

Venice of the Universe
      Ophelia Venice Earth!
        of the Sun's love
        loveliest daughter –
        home of water!

        live!

     if not   with

     in spite of us
     by first our death

The woman I love believes
in God – when I
      seem to blaspheme
             she grieves
    O love! if I as if blaspheme
I worship though I may not yet believe

Only those who will tell home-truths to God
      honour the pride of God
I'll not insult God – behaving as if
God were afraid to face the problem of Evil

Suppose an Almighty unworthy of
    men's best – I'd scorn   Him
but if there is a Lord Whose will is love
I must be frank with Him just as I am
    with my wife whom I love

Is it God's will to let Man's greed end Life?

Come, nuclear fall-out! soft invisible
world-delouser! leave   Earth   scoured
*   _ secure _ restored to*
the peerdom of the lucky planets haughty
circlers for ever, too cold or too hot to
hatch the disease   life . . . Poor sick Earth cured
to bleak purity _ irreversible

And unjust Man presumes to call this 'dirty'!

Was that the word of God at last decided?
God 'saw that it was' bad and God   said
                Let it be cleaned
then turned, and searched the coward galaxies?
                Has searched   Sees?

Again He turns this way and laughs His fiend?

CECILIAL

I listen to some men's music
and hear Godmercy

A keep of honour standing
the long siege   age –

the curbed sortie-longing
the stooping counter-sapping

Iron ration dwindling
the well's level sinking –

honour citadel standing
inside the waiting edge

Strange cargo, eats the ship! – cargo of acid –

runny greed oozing through her bulkheads, nibbling
holes in her ozone skin – bulkheads as thin
as soil, skin rarest air, and the strange thick
proliferating acid
                    eager liquid
blundering bulk gobbling towards self-sinking:

the human cargo growing – its weight shifting –
already Life is dangerously listing

I think perhaps to see things as they are
in the perspective of posterity
may cure the esteem of our self-righteous hatreds.

We need to get Earth's ideological freight
re-distributed – live in amity
with future people stop this worst class-war.

Power is   as many as the Devil

can be   ecstasies of barbarity
clemency for the sake of vanity
addiction to illusions of activity
(must see some fruit from each act even evil)
terror of leisure (it might let in   clarity –
unforesights seen – uninsights antiexcuses
– eerie transparency ambiguity
one's own acts reaching to opponent uses)

and the most subtle of all corruptions charity –
no serving without power therefore win
power or lose your soul! and if   when
won
          slyly the holding loses . . .?
                                        Then –
          then   God is the Devil?

a prayer
for   *the pure in power*

Quick   responsive to the joys
of using power well   being
in the know and action   seeing
            clear   weighing
                  deciding
                  persuading —
make us frisk so
            with — in it all —
the alert pride never to fall
but in   power
                  reject   always
jealousy hatched retaining it
vanity bred displaying it
every   misuse of it
and guard the to some right use of it
      strictly necessary
      lie,
            or cruelty,
clean from any tainting joy

      lie   oneself not truthless
      cruel   never ruthless

The political athlete's good pride
keep us on the stretch keep us fit
                  — us
            fit for power:
            clever and pure

      If Anyone there!
      hear our prayer

O!

Beyond the lunar deathsign
no-ness
blind
fires in flight

The nightmare is
the starry night

As the Sun gives us respite from the stars
(he curtains Earth with light
and we
saved from that sight
are Earth's
only, in Paradise
for the times we call 'days')

– if there is God we do not know

the only name for God is 'O!' –

O!
let us know our luck, so conserve life
even if not ours
garden the world
love
Earth's own
things which leaf

5

Shrinks at the thought of a touch
– or of reclining
                              afraid
        to rest   most

Any breeze a fresh torture

A person has been flayed
                    by a ghost

        of someone future

CRY

Somehow self-respect
without selfrighteousness

The eyes meeting – ours and our successors'

The shame in ours!
      In theirs, hate – by the light
of hate in their eyes we
       seeing their plight

  So then? A remorse wallow?

    Not quite – if they as well are
honest they will know that they'd have done
the murder we are doing
      We-&-they one?
Will – maybe – a dignity of shared shame bless us?

Not for long as we are still possest
of those effects for which
      still their oppressors

   Unless repentance follow

Oh! my offence is ranke, it smels to heaven

unless we cease from doing terracide

    only then earn the pride
to look into those eyes hard and not hide

Cathedral nave lit by the organ-loft

A man alone is improvising – locked
in, in nocturnal strict thought's organ-loft
beacon shelf hung halfwayup sheer rock cliff

The light gropes for the apse – range too long
but clear the dark places echo the fugue
far ones with near – a stretto of mixtures – mocked
he can't find the fugue's end it is lopped off

He has turned and looked east towards the vague

Below – ahead – above: lit from mid-height
the claiming columns, upsurges of arches,
two   triforia, two clerestories of black
windows   and the locking of the vault
recede – pure grandeur few see – straight for night

Flakes of dark have been falling – on my eyes
now   a black snow lies

This Sun – Earth's all – one spangle on Gould's Belt

Aerials catch (in spite of
the veiling waste of light)
a prophecy of dull peril –
the hiss of senile stars
from the prehistory-far
centre of the home spiral

The human dignity?
To be a denizen
of an impurity
in near-all hydrogen

The black snow of the starry skies

And yet a man has felt
in wavebands beside light
the din of his ambition's secret life –

this round Sun's invisible oval
halo – which aerials guided to unveil
by his defiance do reveal

Now the Sun's lusty, the air a mist of milt
dawdling down to a gold dust delta

Beyond a valeful of lit mist
mammal hills   forest-mossed

GLORY

See!   this Sun

outlights the skies'
every star

through being the one
nearest Her

Who bore Him eyes

GUARDIANS

Lift your eyes to the high hills, man –
turn smartly down   look at the soil's fate
What shall we do to be saved? Save   Earth –
help Her to save the green lives while She can:

roots clasping soil – leaves breaking-up brute rain;
the pasture oceans freed from the filth death.
And if   grace of fear makes you ask *Too late?*
lift   your eyes your mind – remember mountains

One breathes a new way in presence of mountains:
air   early with the light among mountains

Even at the instant when you see   snow
on far horizon mountains, the air's new –
white making air fresh from far off   height
a presence in dark lungs They breathe   light

The coming death of Earth
does not invalidate
dolphins   leaves   leafbreath
music's act of faith –

Earth's   coming death
invalidates God –
brute
    quantity
of hydrogen and distance
shrunk
    by quality
having had existence

Earth's final silence is a curse
    which drowns the Universe –
        good
    outroars the stars

Chirp of dolphin
        rustle of leaf
   surf of life
       music's
   hush –
     O could
   the sweet roar
   overtake
     make
every star an ear of God

THE WALK

A clear of evening
             has come
             – the calm,
       the walk home

O twilight   tall sails swift without wind
                       you make

                       the walk
       lead   as if beside a lake
                       toward

a slender stalk and level bloom of smoke

       as if there were a hope

WRAPPED

    After music
           we may go
    through streets and tunnels, carrying
    silences of offering –

        green shot with indigo
        the drake's-head afterglow
    of music
           scarfs us where we go

There is perhaps no God but there are things,
people, times, that are holy – the washed king's
awakening to kneel to his wronged daughter –
cave-walls charged with the light of men encircled
by absolute   dark – and this
                          this work
laid on us by freedom
                  to make men human
at last and virtues (bright forms) hold. O duty
crown!   thorn burning   never consumed!

At a discovery a man's mind stalls:
his full stream crammed back into sudden dalles,
he gathers, in his cloudchamber brain plotting
antics of thought whose waves against the pierced
                 screen of his interposed
doubt   break into particles – paths splitting

Some of the deaf have learned
though also blind
speech
by touch
and Helen Keller heard
by hand
music

Earth! let Your hands of green
be heard be seen
extend
find
if there is God touch
teach
mercy

The want, haunting –
                    again consent to wait –
            conditional guardian angel
                    to live
                    with
                subtle danger
                everywhere

As near to wishful thinking as I dare
I take the consequence of music: give
the act of faith to music – take its word
                    and hear
                            pure the faith
which must be earned by doubting until death

Woman!
    man!
        bind yourself
    your whole life to Earth's life

Each man!
    each woman!
        swear to Earth
    the Hippocratic oath

EXPERIENCE OF BLESSING

Blessings are real, even if God's not:
crushed innocents are, even if God is.
For evil done on / *to* gracious Earth, let
us   have the pride to take on us the curse.

God is men's need of someone they can bless –
Earth-given, the best blessing is this need:
for what She still creates from the Sun's light,
suffering Earth gifts us with thankfulness

which has the grace of rain   not   merely
drops felt falling enfolding thirst with mercy
but seen-from-sunshine rain – how as it passes,
hanging from a stretched cloud which it is partly
dragging downwards, it floats and is bent prettily:
rain-sway – lake-edge water-inverted grasses

Epilogue

I live a double life – have to, am two
                diverging: one of me
      has a feast life
                    the longed-for wife –
my betters' art – myself at latefruit work –
Spring yet again and some still unspoiled walks –
friends – travel – wine (and both of me believe
it's sin not to enjoy blessings we have)
              while the other

recognises this robbed Earth's poison air
      we are bequeathing
                  you to breathe in
and would – my noGod! no! – not live to see
        what we prepare come true

If an agnostic's nearest thing to prayer
has any value
             mine is here for you

JONATHAN GRIFFIN

JONATHAN GRIFFIN was born in Sussex in 1906. He was a journalist and writer on military matters before the Second World War. During the War he was Director of BBC European Intelligence and after the War a diplomat in the Paris embassy. Since 1951 he has devoted himself to writing and translating. He lives in London.

POETRY

The Hidden King (a verse trilogy) Secker & Warburg, 1955
The Rebirth of Pride Secker & Warburg, 1957
The Oath and other poems Giles Gordon, 1962
In Time of Crowding Brookside Press, 1975
In this Transparent Forest Green River Press, 1977
Outsing the Howling Permanent Press, 1979
The Fact of Music The Menard Press, 1980
Commonsense of the Senses The Menard Press, 1983

TRANSLATIONS in book form of the following poets
Camoës (The Menard Press, 1976); Pessoa (Carcanet Press, 1971 and Penguin Books, 1974, reissued with additions, 1982); Char, with M. A. Caws (Princeton University Press, 1976); Jorge de Sena (Mudborn Press, California, 1979); and Jean Mambrino (The Menard Press, 1979).